Kokopelli
ceremonies

Kokopelli
ceremonies

Stephen W. Hill
Illustrations by Robert B. Montoya

KIVA
PUBLISHING, INC.

Library of Congress Catalog Card Number 94-72784

Cataloging-in-Publication Data
Hill, Stephen W.
Kokopelli Ceremonies / Stephen W. Hill ;
illustrations by Robert B. Montoya. — 1st ed.
64 p. cm.
Includes bibliographical references
ISBN 1-885772-05-X (Hardcover)
ISBN 1-885772-06-8 (Softcover)

1. Pueblo Indians—Art   / 2. Pueblo Indians—Legends
3. Kokopelli (Legendary character) / I. Montoya, Robert B., ill   II. Title
E99.P9H55 1995
709'.89'974   QBI94-2196   94-72784

Designed by Steve Marsh
Manufactured in USA

1-95/7.5M/1995

CONTENTS

INTRODUCTION *7*

1 WELLSPRINGS OF CREATIVITY *11*

2 THE ENIGMA OF KOKOPELLI *15*

3 ROBERT MONTOYA, PUEBLO PAINTER JAMES T. BIALAC *29*

4 SPIRITUALITY IN THE ART OF ROBERT B. MONTOYA *31*

5 KOKOPELLI CEREMONIES *37*

A KOKOPELLI BIBLIOGRAPHY *62*

ABOUT THE AUTHOR, ABOUT THE ILLUSTRATOR *64*

LIST OF ILLUSTRATIONS

All illustrations are by Robert B. Montoya. Pen and ink drawings are based on photographs and drawings from various ethnological studies.

10	Standing Flute Player	(from N-M.235, near Cieneguilla)
14	Map of the Four Corners Region, featuring major rock art sites where Kokopelli images are found	
18	Kokopelli as mountain sheep herder	(northeastern Arizona)
20	Kokopelli with insect and lizard	(from Roberts, Bureau of American Ethnology, Bulletin 111)
23	Traditional Hopi Kokopelli Kachina	
27	Kokopelli effigy pitcher	(ca. AD 1000-1150)
32	Deer Night Sky	(courtesy of the author)
33	Emergence from Blue Lake	(courtesy of the artist)
34	The Gathering of the Rain People	(courtesy of the artist)
35	We See Yet Do Not Understand	(courtesy of the artist)
39	Kokopelli's Sunrise Song	(courtesy of the author)
41	Kokopelli's Gift to the Sun	(courtesy of Sam Greenberger)
43	Kokopelli Brothers	(courtesy, private collection)
45	Kokopelli's Sacred Prayers	(courtesy, private collection)
47	Dance of the Kokopelli	(courtesy, private collection)
49	Arrow Priest	(courtesy of the author)
51	Rainbird Priest	(courtesy of the author)
53	Kiva Rain Priest	(courtesy, private collection)
55	Snake Priests	(courtesy of Sam Greenberger)
57	Rain Bearers	(courtesy of Kiva Publishing)
59	Sun Father	(courtesy of Kiva Publishing)
61	Universal Harmony	(courtesy of the artist)
64	Stephen W. Hill	(photograph by Louis Martinez)
	Robert B. Montoya	(photograph by Murrae Haynes)

INTRODUCTION

The inspiration for this book came directly from the work of Robert Montoya. In early 1993, I had an opportunity to study several paintings from his Kokopelli series, including "Rainbird Priest" (illustrated in this book). The images and titles made such a strong impression that I contacted Bob to ask him if he had produced additional Kokopelli paintings and to inquire into the stories behind the paintings.

As a student of Pueblo painting, I was arrested by the originality of the style, but at the same time I caught hints of the familiar. Was it the figure of Kokopelli kindling my imagination, or was it perhaps some resemblance to the abstract geometries of Joe Herrera, Helen Hardin, and Tony Da, other Pueblo painters whose work I admired? Maybe the excitement generated by Montoya's Kokopelli originated from a deeper source, such as the energies behind the pre-Columbian roots of Kokopelli's image pecked and painted on rock surfaces throughout the Four Corners. Or perhaps there was something archetypal in the multiple manifestations of this "hero with a thousand faces."

The idea of a multifaceted mythological hero deserved further exploration, for my initial researches on Kokopelli had revealed that historical depictions of the Humpback Flute Player and the meanings ascribed to him were extremely diverse, sometimes even contradictory. In various texts and articles, I encountered him as a hunter, a warrior, a musician, a fertility god, a deformed individual, and even an insect! Could it be that Kokopelli was a kind of trickster-hero, derived from a variety of sources, and invested with absurd deformity on one hand, but creativity and power on the other, similar to the fool in a Shakespeare play? Both the ethnographic record and Montoya's renditions suggested this interpretation.

In the paintings, there is no contradiction or "cognitive dissonance" in depicting Kokopelli as Rain Priest or Sun Father, as praying or dancing, as singular or plural. Montoya is free to present numerous identities sometimes attributed to Kokopelli and others from his own imagination, without the need to settle on one. And yet one element all Montoya's representations have in common is the sacred or priestly role. This priestlike personage is in some ways similar to the creative artist, who engenders diversity and harmony from the fabric of his or her chosen medium. The ceremonial or ritual aspect of this artistic act of creation and celebration is embodied in the geometric forms and blending of colors within the paintings.

Thus Robert Montoya's series of paintings depicting Kokopelli as celebrant formed the inspirational core for a book to be titled **Kokopelli Ceremonies.** But here I encountered a problem: it wouldn't make sense to showcase Robert Montoya's work without some commentary, both on the paintings themselves and on Kokopelli. Should this be an art book, a book on Native American spirituality, a review of the literature on Kokopelli? When I interviewed Montoya on the sources of his inspiration for the paintings, it became evident that this book would have to be a hybrid. Since no comprehensive survey of the research and opinions about Kokopelli was yet available, investigating and presenting that background would be an essential task. (Slifer and Duffield's **Kokopelli: Flute Player Images in Rock Art,** which was published shortly before this book was completed, documents ancient images comprehensively and makes a good case for the multiple identities of the historical Kokopelli.)

As the stories behind the paintings emerged, the spirituality informing the art became increasingly apparent. The vitality and appeal of much Native American art, whether contemporary or historical, is deeply embedded in its spiritual significance. Robert Montoya's paintings are no exception. Even without commentary, the compositions themselves present that holistic vision, which is the inspiration and guiding spirit for this book.

Ethnologists might be interested in tracking Kokopelli to his point of origin, or in determining his original identity. On the other hand, I am attracted by the variety of his roles and by the ambiguity behind his personality. Thus Chapter One, "Wellsprings of Creativity," presents a rationale for looking beyond the logical categories of ethnology and anthropology to the holistic experiencing typically regarded as "right brain."

The research section of this book, Chapter Two, "The Enigma of Kokopelli," emphasizes the possibilities rather than the probabilities in an attempt to understand Kokopelli as a diverse rather than consistent character. Because his figure is readily appropriated by the popular imagination, I have chosen to explore his meaning and his appeal in light of the human tendency to project and create multiple meanings, often ignoring the facts. I have no argument with those who seek to build positions on the facts and no intention of obscuring the conclusions drawn by others. On the other hand, the scientific method, which forms judgments based on fine discriminations and logical categories ("either/or" thinking) is only one way to examine a phenomenon such as Kokopelli. An altogether different light is shed on the subject by studying the perhaps irrational conclusions drawn by the imagination from internal experience and then playing with the possibilities. That is the method of Chapter Two.

Chapter Three, "Robert Montoya, Pueblo Painter," is a brief introduction to the artist. I asked Jim Bialac to introduce Bob because as a collector Jim has a truly broad perspective on Native American painting in the Southwest. Rarely is a major book written or a major retrospective exhibit of Navajo or Pueblo painting given without Jim's generous participation, usually in the form of a loan from his extensive collection. A member of the Editorial Advisory Board of **American Indian Art** and a trustee of the Heard Museum, Jim Bialac is truly a patron of the arts, who through his taste in collecting has influenced the "collectibility" of many painters. He has followed the career of Bob Montoya since the early 1970's, and was a collector of Bob's work long before the general public knew of Bob's reputation.

Chapter Four, "Spirituality in the Art of Robert Montoya," introduces the artist as a Native American and as a painter. Robert Montoya is no exception to the proverbial widom that art is not a separate category for Native Americans, but just another expression of spiritual being. Whereas "easel painting" in the Southwest is a relatively recent phenomenon, the Pueblos have used painting ceremonially and spiritually as far back as historical artifacts can be traced. It is evident from the Kokopelli paintings and the artist's explanations that his artistic and spiritual concerns are one.

The paintings themselves and commentary on them form the substance of Chapter Five, "Kokopelli Ceremonies." The explanatory notes are not intended as explications of the paintings, but rather as background, providing some details of Pueblo culture that may be helpful in understanding the artist's intent. These commentaries are collaborations based on my interviews with Robert Montoya, and as such reflect both his sensibility and my own poetic license.

The bibliography is intended to give credit to research sources and to direct the reader to more detailed information than this book provides. As a student fascinated by Kokopelli, I welcome facts, opinions, and stories which are not included in the present work as well as correspondence about the theories already presented. I may be contacted through Kiva Publishing.

I am grateful to the librarians and aides at the Heard Museum and the Southwest Museum for their support in my research efforts. My wife, Ronni, and my daughter, Elizabeth, supported me as I stole time from them to struggle with concepts, research and writing. I am most appreciative of the suggestions and encouragement given by Ronni and by Andy Hoye, who read the manuscript and assisted with refinements.

In a very fundamental way, this book is a collaborative enterprise. Every step of the way, Bob Montoya and I coordinated efforts, prodding and encouraging one another, sharing views and enjoying one another's company. I feel honored to present to a broader audience an artist whose creativity and vision are so consistent with his personality.

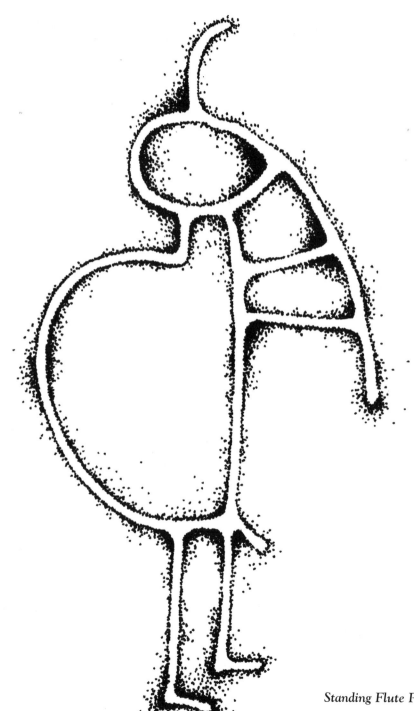

Standing Flute Player (from Cieneguilla site N-M.235)

WELLSPRINGS OF CREATIVITY

The marriage of psychology, religion and art, an unquestioned and very natural assumption in Native American cultures, continues to struggle for acknowledgment in Anglo-European civilization. The categories by which the dominant culture in the West understands and presents creative experience indicate that these three fields are often seen as separate, without common roots. For example, bookstores present art as a series of monographs, psychology as self-help, and religion as discrete belief systems of East and West.

By contrast, it is often very difficult to separate the creative and artistic productions of Native Americans and other indigenous peoples from their roots in religion, psychology and daily life. Indeed, in many of these cultures, the native language does not even have a word for "art."

Western culture has not always been so fragmented. In the Middle Ages, psychology did not exist as a separate category, and painting was often a form of religious devotion. Even in modern times, prominent twentieth century thinkers in the Western tradition have emphasized the connections that unify these fields. Sigmund Freud, for example, alluded to the ancient Greek drama's spiritual capacity to reduce psychological tension. C.G. Jung emphasized the common archetypal core at the heart of spiritual and psychological experience, and encouraged his patients to express their growth holistically through drawing and painting. And Joseph Campbell, in his studies of folklore and mythology, uncovered universal spiritual and psychological needs as well as common structures in tales from around the world. Thus, despite the separations so often apparent in descriptions of religion, psychology and art, Western tradition has sometimes acknowledged that these categories share a common root. Despite the message from Western thinkers to consider the common source of art and spirituality in the creativity of the human psyche, Western culture continues to struggle uncomfortably with holistic thinking. Perhaps the influence of linear, rational thought on industrial and technological success has predisposed us to focus on production rather than process. Maybe the myth of endless progress has captured our souls so that we deny evidence to the contrary. At any rate, the dominant cultures within our global village have brought the world to an impasse where "koyaanisqatsi" (Hopi for "world out of balance") accurately describes our dilemma.

While the arts and crafts of native cultures worldwide have continued to reflect harmony, closeness to nature, balance and simplicity, the arts of dominant cultures are more likely to express angst, irony and ennui than to celebrate the spiritual. And yet the impulse behind these apparently contradictory expressions of creativity is fundamentally the same: to manifest the needs of the human spirit.

For instance, in the modern era, much of the most influential art of the dominant culture has opposed the legacy of unrelenting material progress. Nearly a hundred years ago, in 1896, Alfred Jarry's *Ubu Roi* scandalized Paris audiences by presenting a rude and boorish buffoon as king, in his mad rush for power sweeping away all that was elegant, refined and orderly. A short time later, in 1913, Stravinski's *Le Sacre du Printemps* caused a riot by presenting harsh dissonance and primitive rhythms that appeared to some listeners to undermine the Western classical tradition of music.

And yet the apparent disharmony of these and other works of modern art underlies a fundamental human need to express truths about the human condition, no matter how painful. By the dawn of the twentieth century, Western artists had become acutely aware of the fragmentation and discord within their culture and civilization. A world out of joint was reflected in the art of the surrealists, dadaists, cubists and expressionists.

The history of Anglo-European civilization has also witnessed a split between science and religion, where the discoveries of science have increasingly banished religion to an otherworldly realm, as if evolution and creation could not be part of the same reality. For indigenous peoples there is no such contradiction. Historically for Native Americans, stories and legends have been naturally accepted not as scientific evidence, but as spiritual truths. In rituals and ceremonies, they pray for and celebrate the harmonious balance of humans, animals and natural forces. Arts such as painting, song and dance are an integral part of religious and spiritual culture.

The appeal to Westerners of Native American art, both ancient and modern, is not surprising. Artworks reflecting harmony, balance and communal values have a strong

fascination for a civilization where, in the words of W. B. Yeats, "Things fall apart; the center cannot hold;/ Mere anarchy is loosed upon the world." Artists whose sensibilities are tuned to the fragmentation and discord of the modern world continue to yearn for the experience of wholeness. T. S. Eliot's classic depictions of the disharmony of modern life in *The Waste Land* and "The Hollow Men" are echoed in "Burnt Norton," in which he describes a "place of disaffection" where "strained time-ridden faces" are "distracted from distraction by distraction." Yet deep within that experience he identifies a central core where all is in balance, the "still point of the turning world." Whether a creative artist chooses to express the chaos of the world or its harmonies, the impulse to create springs from the same source.

However much we attempt to categorize and rationalize the products of the human imagination, we inevitably encounter a singular obstacle: the fountain of creativity is infinite, and the variations on any given theme are endless. Indeed, creative production is a continuum where orderliness and randomness alternate. The appearance of Kokopelli is a case in point. In ancient times, he appeared in various roles on rock surfaces. He may have been etched there by shamans and priests as a deity or power figure, or he may have been represented as he actually appeared in daily life. Though his image has been identified throughout the Four Corners, he appears in many transformations: sometimes phallic, sometimes not; playing a flute, carrying a staff, or swallowing an arrow; arched or humpbacked, with or without a headdress; singly, in pairs, or in groups; associated with love or war. Is Kokopelli a variation on a theme, or does he, in fact, embody numerous interrelated themes?

The questions may be taken a step further. Is rock art a religious enterprise, or is it an expression of communal psychology? Could it be both, and at the same time a highly pleasing aesthetic object resonating with an archetypal energy that we all share as humans? If we begin to understand Kokopelli's ancient and modern appeal as a function simultaneously of aesthetic, spiritual, and psychological impulses, we can form a bridge to the ancients through our appreciation of his modern manifestations. Robert Montoya's paintings of Kokopelli, featured in this book, are one creative artist's variations on a theme that has captivated imaginations for thousands of years. As an artist of Native American heritage and culture educated within the dominant Anglo-European culture, he is uniquely positioned to share his vision of the Humpback Flute Player.

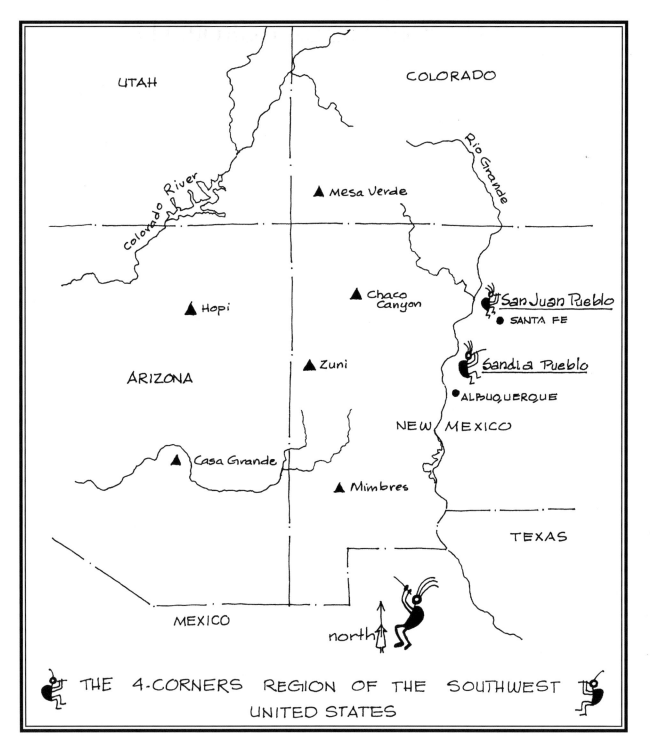

THE 4-CORNERS REGION OF THE SOUTHWEST
UNITED STATES

14

THE ENIGMA OF KOKOPELLI

Visitors to the Four Corners (New Mexico, Arizona, Colorado and Utah), a region noted for natural wonders, spirituality and art, often tell of the extraordinary impression left by figures from Native American folklore and religion. Rainbirds, parrots and fetish bears populate paintings, pottery and jewelry. Coyotes howl from menus and T-shirts. A wide array of Hopi kachinas assembles for inspection in museums and storefronts. The graceful Eagle Dancer and the playful striped Koshare dance in the imagination. But among the images of the Southwest pantheon, no figure has evoked such widespread interest and popular appeal as the omnipresent Kokopelli.

Also known as the Humpbacked Flute Player, Kokopelli appears in contexts ancient and modern, from petroglyphs on the cliff walls of Chaco Canyon to iron sculptures in the front yards of Santa Fe residents. He is depicted on trail markers for the hiker and commercial signs of public businesses, as if he were somehow an emblem of the region itself. Visitors to his Southwest home are almost certain to take back with them a bit of lore or a story about this musically-named character who is most commonly recognized by his Hopi name.

In the Four Corners, Kokopelli has for many years been an intriguing subject of investigation and speculation. Anthropologists, archaeologists and ethnologists have studied his many representations on cliffs and canyon walls.

Among the Pueblos, Zunis and Hopis, he appears in rituals and ceremonies. Even medical doctors have joined the chorus of commentators, suggesting he was a historical person and theorizing about the possible diseases accounting for his disability. Storytellers from Pueblo elders to Tony Hillerman have entertained listeners by portraying the humpback in folktales and myths. And artists—painters, potters, jewelers and sculptors—have depicted Kokopelli in forms as diverse as the theories about him.

Why does Kokopelli have such universal recognition and evoke such fascination? Clearly he was important in the pantheon of the Anasazi (ancestors of the Pueblos), for he appears more frequently than any other identifiable figure in petroglyphs and pictographs near the sites of ancient settlements. Yet his current popularity extends far beyond the Pueblos. He has caught the interest of countless visitors to the Southwest, thereby transcending his ancient meanings to become a luminary of a broader and more contemporary mythology.

In recent years, his popularity has gained him the status of a symbol or archetype, appealing as he does to the popular imagination. Thus Kokopelli takes on meanings beyond those ascribed by ethnological studies and religious beliefs. Barton Wright (1993) recognizes this phenomenon when he says, "It seems...likely that the original Hump-backed Flute Player, in more recent times, has been combined with other individuals that are superficially similar, creating today's aggregation of beings all conveniently labeled 'Kokopelli.'"

KOKOPELLI'S UNIVERSALITY

Perhaps Kokopelli's universality is nothing new, and his presence in the Southwest is only one of many incarnations. Anthropologist Dr. Alfred Kidder has discovered hump-backed figures in northern Mexico, suggesting that this image is found among Toltec or Aztec peoples, perhaps as a depiction of the trader known as puchteca. Elsie Clews Parsons, who favors the theory that Kokopelli is an insect, infers that insects are important spirits not only to the Rio Grande Pueblos, but to other Mesoamerican cultures, including the Aztecs.

On the other hand, his pervasive appeal may be due less to historical factors than to the vital nature of his roles. Whether through rock art, storytelling, or ritualistic enactment, Kokopelli is usually portrayed engaging in activities basic to human life, such as hunting, bringing boons (trade items, babies, seeds, rain), sexuality, music and dance, and healing.

Somehow the harmonious interplay of these fundamental facets of human existence is captured in the figure who is almost universally depicted as humpbacked, typically carries a flute, cane, or staff, sometimes sports a large phallus, and often is pictured with antennae or feathers on his head, and occasionally a clubfoot. Like the wise fool in Shakespeare, his deformity belies his worth, and like the trickster heroes in many Native American cultures, his imperfection is inseparable from the benefits he brings. He represents both bane and boon, disability and healing, humor and high seriousness, and who he is cannot be distinguished from the dance he performs. Small wonder, then, that he has captured the imaginations of the ancients, the Pueblo people of today, and innumerable visitors to the Southwest where his image is so commonly found.

Perhaps so many of us respond to Kokopelli because he reaches us on many levels. Not only does he serve a communal and psychological need through his essential activities, but he also answers an aesthetic need through sheer visual presentation. As the bringer of fertility to humans and their crops, as medicine man or trader, he sat-isfies a practical requirement. And as a dancing, flute-play-ing, circular celebrant, he is the Ian Anderson of the Pueblos, the Pied Piper of the Rio Grande, reaching into the unconscious core where the senses are joined, fulfilling our root need to integrate and harmonize the fragments of our existence.

WHO IS KOKOPELLI?

Diversity is a hallmark of the Humpbacked Flute Player. His history, as gathered from petroglyphs and pictographs, legends and stories, and modern day religious enactments, displays him in many roles, both sacred and profane. Unlike Coyote, he is not universally regarded as a trickster, yet his various portrayals revolve around his capacity to enhance the life of the people, whether through bringing rain or producing babies, hunting sheep or bearing gifts. Kokopelli's many roles suggest that he is a shapeshifter, adapting to a variety of human needs by taking on different guises.

LEGENDS OF KOKOPELLI AS TRADER, GAMBLER, OR MINSTREL

Puchteca

It is evident from the appearance in the Rio Grande area of items characteristic of central Mexico, such as parrot and macaw feathers, pyrite mirrors, and copper bells, that traders from Mexico frequented the Pueblos. The Aztec or Toltec trader, known as *puchteca,* bears a pack of goods on his back and carries a cane or walking stick. He is sometimes shown carrying a flute to announce his arrival, presumably so that he will not be seen as an enemy. Wearing a backpack and playing the flute, the *puchteca* would certainly etch the image of a Kokopelli-like figure into the consciousness of the people he encountered. Did Kokopelli derive his reputation as bringer of gifts from these traders who brought fascinating items from faraway lands, or did the appearance of the *puchteca* simply embellish the already considerable prestige of the humpback?

Nepokwai-i

The Hopi-Tewa, who came from the Rio Grande area to live among the Hopi at First Mesa, tell of a large black trader, whom they refer to as Nepokwai-i. On his back he bears a large sack of buckskins, which he uses to make moccasins for young women. Some have speculated that the prototype for this figure may have been Esteban, a Moor who served as a scout in 1539 for the exploration party of Friar Marcos de Niza.

Even today, Pueblos often say that the first white man their ancestors saw was a black man, referring to the flamboyant scout whose appearance must have made a startling impression: this gigantic man had an entourage of females whom he had received as gifts from the natives as he travelled towards Zuni, and he wore colorful feathers and bells on his wrists, and a plumed crown on his head. The story goes that upon entering the Zuni village of Hawikuh, Esteban was set upon and murdered, for he had angered the elders by demanding presents and women.

Notwithstanding his untimely demise, the impact of Esteban's stature, color and confidence as he passed through several villages may have given him legendary merit. Furthermore, his crown of plumes ties in very nicely with Kokopelli's typical headdress, and the cadre of women would certainly emphasize his sexual potency. Since it is impossible to accurately trace the development of the legendary figure Nepokwai'i, we are left with a conjecture. Perhaps the impression left by the Moor has contributed to the legend of Nepokwai-i, who resembles Kokopelli by the sack on his back and his reputation as a bringer of boons.

Gambler

One tale that has been recounted by the Navajos, the Zuni, and as far west as Acoma, concerns a gambler and his companion, a humpbacked flute player. The Navajo version of the story tells of Blue Feather, a Zuni who was proficient at throwing sticks. Through his skill, he wins the entire treasure of Pueblo Bonito and attempts to take over ruling power. His hubris leads him to the sacrilegious act of marrying a maiden dedicated to the gods, bringing the gods' anger upon the city. In the disease, drought, and famine that follow, both he and his humpbacked companion, who is arguably the symbolic representation of his disease, perish.

In a more comic version of the story, the humpbacked flute player survives and lives happily ever after with the maiden. The variable fate of the humpback in these tales suggests that, like the trickster-heroes (such as coyote and rabbit), he represents impulsive creativity, which may lead to positive or negative results. As companion to a gambler, the humpback may win or lose, depending on the path he takes.

Minstrel

Among the Pueblo people, Kokopelli sometimes appears in legends and stories as a musician. The flute evidently had a special role in Anasazi culture, and today it is still associated with fertility rituals. One story from San Ildefonso presents him as a wandering minstrel carrying a sack of songs on his back, trading new songs for old. In other tales, he is

Kokopelli as a mountain sheep herder (from northeastern Arizona)

seen as a god of the harvest and a flute-playing bringer of fertility. This portrait is consistent with the Pueblo ceremonial emphasis on music and dance to reflect and influence harmony with nature.

Kokopelli's Symbolic and Spiritual Roles
Hunter or Warrior

Depicted in some petroglyphs in northern Arizona and New Mexico as a hunter with bow and arrow, Kokopelli may have used a flute to draw the curious mountain sheep within hunting range. In numerous petroglyphs, mountain sheep are found in groups, pursued by hunters, sometimes playing a flute, sometimes bending over, holding a bow.

The Navajo tell stories of mountain sheep carrying on their backs clouds containing seeds of many types of vegetation. This iconographic description is not very far from the reality that the sheep do catch up in their wool bits of the vegetation they travel through, including seeds, which must sometimes drop off to effectively disperse the range of certain plants. In that sense, the mountain sheep are also bringers of fertility, mirroring the role of Kokopelli the hunter.

A similar correspondence is suggested by the Navajo god Ganaskidi, whose hump also represents a cloud and is filled with produce from the fields. The Ganaskidi ("Ganaskidi" means "humpback") are said to be a numerous race of divinities who often appear to humans as Rocky Mountain sheep. Like Kokopelli, they are gods of plenty and harvest gods. In ceremonies, this deity resembles Kokopelli more than just superficially: his crown, made of a basket, is decorated with radiating feathers to represent the sun's rays emerging from the edge of a cloud. His cloud bag is so heavy that he must bend his back and lean on a staff.

The identification of Ganaskidi with the Mountain Sheep poses an intriguing question. Is there any meaningful difference between Ganaskidi of the Mountain Sheep people and Kokopelli the hunter of mountain sheep? Logically there is, but in the Pueblo and Navajo ceremonial worlds where the dancers' costumes and headdresses resemble the hunted animal, this correspondence signifies the harmonious intertwining of human and animal worlds. The dance ritual portrays and supplicates not only the fertility and propagation of the animal, but also its cooperation in the hunt, where the hunters will take only what they need for food. Logically, the the hunter and the hunted are separated, but in the ritual they are one.

Hunters depicted in petroglyphs appear sometimes as single figures, sometimes in a group. They occasionally carry bow and arrow. Some groups of figures with shapes reminiscent of Kokopelli are shown dancing together, possibly performing a hunt ritual or ceremonial war dance. Without knowing more of the history of the spiritual beliefs and practices of the Anasazi, we can only infer from our present understanding of Pueblo ceremonies that this ceremonial dancing, whether preparatory to the hunt or war, is intended to enhance the success of the activity that follows.

God, Priest or Sacred Musician

Another Navajo god who bears some similarity to Kokopelli is To'nenili ("Water Sprinkler"). The potent water of this deity consists of "he-rain, she-rain, hail, snow, lake water, spring water and water taken from the four quarters of the world." (Matthews, 1897) In legends, he is found accompanying Hastsezini (the god of fire), Ganaskidi, and Hastse'oltoi (divine huntress). These four divinities, representing fire, water, hunting and harvest, embody elemental forces essential to human survival in a hunter-gatherer economy. To'nenili, who is clearly associated with fertility, sometimes leads ceremonies, bent over and sprinkling water from his water bag. He also appears in a clownlike role at the end of the Yeibechai Ceremony, making fun and playing tricks.

Could Kokopelli be a priest? Many Kokopelli figures are shown wearing long and gracefully curved feathers on their heads, in the characteristic dress of priests. The Zuni often describe Kokopelli as a Rain Priest, and they state that his frequent depiction in petroglyphs represents supplication for rain in this arid region where the people are intensely dependent on the infrequent and sometimes unpredictable rain for their very sustenance. Indeed, the name "Kokopelli" is evidently of compound origin, with "koko"

in the Zuni language translated as either "rain people" or "kachina," and "pelli" (polo) in Hopi meaning "hemisphere" or "hump."

According to Frank Roberts, Jr., an archaeologist who in 1932 reported on humpbacked flute players found in petroglyphs dated 1000-1030 A.D., the Zuni "call the flute player figure Chu'lu'laneh, the name for the type of flute used by the rain priests" (Roberts, 1932). Two figures from the contemporary Zuni pantheon, both appearing during the corn-grinding ceremony, also resemble Kokopelli— Paiyatumu, who arrives playing the flute, and Olowishkya, a phallic figure.

Most rock art representations of Kokopelli show him playing a long, direct flute or flageolet. Most often, he is blowing through one end and holding the flute with both hands, typically with the flute inclined downwards, though sometimes it is horizontal, and more rarely (in northeast Arizona) upwards. Kokopelli's role as a flute-playing priest is difficult to separate from his more secular role as a minstrel, for Pueblo and Navajo spirituality is close to the heart of everyday living. Historically, Native Americans have played the flute for a variety of reasons: not only to accompany a variety of religious ceremonies, some of which ask for rain to nurture good crops or summer flowers; but also to demonstrate musical prowess or stimulate romantic interest.

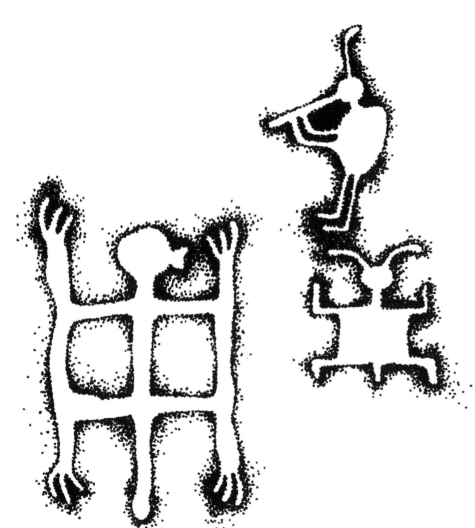

Kokopelli with insect and lizard
(from Roberts, Bureau of American Ethnology, Bulletin 111)

INSECT OR MEDICINE MAN

One of the most unusual but most adamantly argued theories about Kokopelli is that he is an insect. In the Four Corners area, along the San Juan River, many images render a humpbacked flute-playing figure lying on its back, legs in the air. From its head emerge two antennae, either straight or in a lightning-like zigzag.

Elsie Clews Parsons in 1938 asserted firmly that "the humpbacked flute player of the rock walls and potsherds is so obviously an insect, 'once you see it,' that no analysis is called for." For corroboration, she calls on the observations of J.W. Fewkes, who studied Hopi culture for many years, and who alluded to Kokopelli as "a certain dipterous insect" (Fewkes, 1903). She refers to Kokopelli's representation in company with other insects in pictographs near the Village of the Great Kivas, and suggests strongly that Locust, who has been represented playing the flute on Hopi Flute Society altar tiles, is his most likely identity.

Indeed, Locust, the patron of Hopi Flute societies, is in charge of both music and healing. Locust medicine is used by the Hopis for treating wounds, since Locust is seen as impervious to lightning bolts. In one version of the Hopi Emergence myth, Locust is sent from the underworld to scout for an exit to the upper world. As he arrives, the Clouds shoot lightning bolts through him, but he just continues playing his flute. In another version of the myth, Locust dies after being shot with arrows, but he resurrects.

Therefore Locust represents powerful medicine that can cure lightning shock and arrow wounds.

Hopi Flute societies have locust medicine to aid in premonitory dreaming, and he is also considered to have the capacity to bring warm weather. In one Hopi folk tale, the Snakes appeal to the Locusts to assist in melting the snow, and they do so by playing their flutes and singing of the approaching summer. Surely the powers represented as being Locust's, together with his humpback and his flute, make a compelling case for his identity as Kokopelli (and vice versa).

Fertility Kachina

Marjorie Lambert (1957) hypothesizes from archaelogical and ethnological evidence that "the God of Fire and the Humpbacked Flute Player could very well be the oldest in concept among the archaelogical supernaturals" whose "magical powers are still recognized, particularly with reference to rainfall, and crop, and human fertility." Etienne Renaud (1948) emphasizes that "what survives today is only a fraction of the rich mythology of past centuries, and possibly even adulterated in part by the contact with the Catholic faith tending to submerge the ancestral belief."

The Hopi kachina known as Kuwaan Kokopelli is also known as the Colored Assassin or Robber Fly Kachina. The robber fly is a predatory insect with a humped back and long proboscis that steals the larvae of other flies and is constantly copulating. Kuwaan Kokopelli is one of the fertility or copulation kachinas, and he has his own song and dance. Sometimes during ceremonies he borrows a flute from the Flute Kachina and plays it.

However, Kokopelli's depiction and his role vary from village to village, even within the Hopi mesas. For example, at Shungopavi (Second Mesa), he is a humpback flute player to whom the people can pray for anything they want. He wears a shirt and carries seeds in his hump. At Old Oraibi (Third Mesa), on the other hand, he carries not a flute but a cane, and also a rattle, and has flowers atop his head.

Hopi tradition also includes a sister kachina, Kokopell' Mana. The behavior of this character is consistent with the Hopi predilection to appreciate the humorous side of sexuality. In the springtime, Kokopell' Mana (always a man dressed as a woman) is one of the "racing kachinas" who appear during the spring dances to challenge the men of the village. Usually one of the faster runners of the village takes this role. If Kokopell' Mana catches the man she has challenged, she tackles him and mounts him, imitating copulation. Of course, an audience of interested villagers howls appreciatively at these antics. If she loses the race, she rewards the man with somipiki, made of cornmush wrapped in cornhusks.

While there is great fun in the shenanigans of the runner

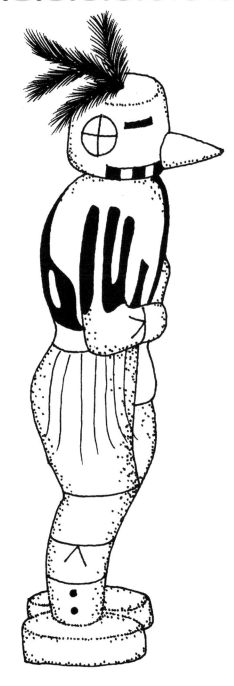

Kokopelli kachina from Shipaulovi
(from Hawley, American Anthropologist, 1937). (The Kokopelli Kachina is also fre-
quently seen with a more prominent hump and the snout pointed upward.)

kachinas, there are also clear overtones of a spring fertility rite in the behavior of Kokopell' Mana; furthermore, the reward and punishment involved imitates the natural consequences of the race of life. There is probably also a broader spiritual purpose to the races, for some Hopis say that racing stimulates rain and restores some of the energy the earth has provided.

Hopi legends about Kokopelli portray him as bearing gifts in a backpack, with which he seduces girls by holding up desirable items to draw them near. When they are close enough, he chases them but often fails to catch them. More sedate stories describe him as bearing babies on his back, which he leaves with young women. Clearly, the notion of Kokopelli as a fertility figure is accommodated by both these descriptions.

Though many of the older representations of Kokopelli, particularly rock art, show him as phallic, more recent and contemporary versions rarely include his notable member. This omission is probably a legacy of the Spanish missionaries, who brought a more repressed vision of appropriateness and decency to the Pueblos. On the other hand, the appreciation of fertility symbolism and the absurdity and humor of sexuality is not lost to the Hopi and the Pueblos, for these features of life continue to be presented in Pueblo life during ceremonies by such figures as Kokopelli, Kokopell' Mana, and the clowning Koshares.

Realistic Explanations

When the mind is not satisfied with explanations that involve spiritual significance and symbolism, it often turns to realism as a way to explain observations. Like any other enigmatic or imperfectly explained character, Kokopelli has drawn advocates of various realistic explanations. Thus we have speculations based on history; for example, that Kokopelli's humpbacked form and his function as a bringer of gifts is really based on observance of puchtecas from central Mexico, or, alternately, that Esteban the Moor with his plumed crown and harem afforded a godlike image of fertility that later took shape as Nepokwai'i.

Another fascinating approach to realistic understanding is provided by medical explanations for Kokopelli's humpbacked condition. Joyce Alpert theorizes that Kokopelli may have been "an actual disabled individual who was important in the prehistory of the Southwest." (1991) It is indeed possible to evaluate certain rock art portrayals of Kokopelli as a victim of Pott's disease (tuberculosis of the spine), for they display some or all of the salient symptoms: kyphosis (exaggerated posterior convexity), chest abnormality, priapism (permanent erection), and foot abnormality (such as clubfoot).

It is commonly assumed that much rock art was carefully executed as a part of ceremony or ritual, hence the render-ing of these features can be assumed to be deliberate. Because Pueblo culture traditionally rejected unusual-appearing individuals, such a deformed person, in order to be accepted, would have to present special attributes perceived as beneficial by the group, such as fertility. While the correspondence between Pott's disease and Kokopelli's features is intriguing, the argument that Kokopelli was an actual person accounts for only a few of the variations in his portrayal.

Kokopelli in Ancient Art

Petroglyphs and Pictographs

When referring to "art" created within Native American cultures, it is important to understand that representations of human and animal figures, whether painted or pecked on canyon walls, embodied in pottery or sculpted forms, designed as beadwork or weaving, or presented as music and dance, most often has a ceremonial or ritualistic purpose, and sometimes also a practical use, not merely an aesthetic one. Ancient and modern Native American artists and artisans from the Southwest recognize a correspondence between what is portrayed in artistic form and the needs of the human spirit. Thus, the Western European tradition of "art" as objects or performances designed for the enjoyment and appreciation of the viewer, on one hand overstates the intended use of much Native American art, and on the other hand, understates its spiritual significance.

Petroglyphs (incised or pecked figures) and pictographs (figures painted or drawn in chalk or colored pigments) are the earliest known representations of Kokopelli, dated by ethnologists from 200 A.D. through the sixteenth century. While "rock art" did not stop at that point, the adulteration of the Pueblo cultures through exposure to the Spanish explorers, missionaries and conquistadores becomes evident in the juxtaposition of Kokopelli and other earlier forms with cowled men and armored men on horseback.

The meaning or purpose these petroglyphs and pictographs had for those who drew them is purely a matter of conjecture, since no record of either a written language or a system of hieroglyphics exists, and oral tradition does not present any meaningful explanation. According to Weaver (1984),

> most of the prehistoric rock art of the Colorado Plateau has been interpreted by scientists as attempts to propitiate supernatural forces and to insure individual or group prosperity. Thus, the rock art itself is directly or indirectly related to ceremonial and religious activities. Specific functions within this general interpretation range from sympathetic hunting magic to requests for rain, from depictions of clan ancestors...to specific designs believed to foster fertility, good health, power, and success in hunting.

The Humpbacked Flute Player has been portrayed on rock faces and canyon walls in numerous locations in the Southwest, observed by many ethnographic and archaelogical expeditions. In 1919, Kidder and Guernsey came across Kokopelli as a hunter of mountain sheep among petroglyphs studied near Hagoe Canyon in northeastern Arizona. Roberts, in 1932, discovered the figure of a humpbacked flute player in association with a horntoad and an unidentified insect in a prehistoric (1000-1030 A.D.) Pueblo site near Zuni. He hypothesized that the toad and insect were supposed to aid the flute player in attracting clouds and moisture to the area.

One of the most extensive studies of petroglyphs was done in 1938, in an expedition led by Etienne Renaud. The group he led studied petroglyphs at twenty sites in north-central New Mexico. Their attention was attracted by the frequency and appearance of the Kokopelli figure, which was found at five of the twenty sites explored by his party. The greatest number of representations appeared in Cieneguilla, south of Santa Fe, where Kokopelli appears in his various roles as flutist, hunter, warrior, dancer and priest.

Numerous photographs and sketches from this expedition indicate that the Humpbacked Flute Player is depicted in many varied configurations, even within the same geographical area. Renaud's article includes drawings depicting Kokopelli in association with Avanyu the sacred water serpent, with groups of hunters or warriors, in insect-like poses, and even rendered in extremely abstract form.

More recently, Slifer and Duffield (1994) completed an extensive study of rock art depictions of Kokopelli, documenting his remarkably varied appearances in New Mexico, Arizona, Utah and Colorado. Their amply illustrated research presents valuable historical and geographical findings which serve to amplify the conclusions of past students of Kokopelli, particularly his lack of consistent form and function.

Pottery, Effigies, Kiva Murals

Although human or anthropomorphic portrayals on prehistoric pottery is extremely rare in the northern Rio Grande area, fragments of pottery and some whole pieces feature Kokopelli within their decorations. His image has also been recognized in pre-Columbian effigies and as an element of kiva murals.

One of the oldest and most carefully studied representations of Kokopelli comes from an effigy pitcher discovered in northwestern New Mexico, southwest of Chaco Canyon, dating from approximately 1000-1150 A.D. The black-on-white vessel is unusual in combining a large bird-form pitcher with many of the attributes of Kokopelli modeled and painted on it. The pitcher itself combines a bird shape with the figure of a flute player, arms extended to hold a flute, which is the handle. Two figures painted in the chest area, extending downward from the shoulders, appear to represent male and female Kokopellis. Viewed from the side, the vessel apparently displays Kokopelli lying on his back, with the underside intended to illustrate the humped back.

Marjorie Lambert (1967) theorizes that this prehistoric Humpbacked Flute Player is ancestral to the modern Kokopelli and Nepokwa'i. In the form of the pitcher she traces Mesoamerican influence, and she concludes that the vessel was most likely used in rites and ceremonies associated with fertility, considering Kokopelli's identification with hunting, rain, and fecundity of plant and animal life.

An intriguing speculation emerges in Lambert's (1957) discussion of a stone effigy unearthed at Pecos Pueblo. The humpbacked figurine has features in common with both the Fire God and Kokopelli as well as with effigies discovered in Mexico.

Lambert proposes:
> It may be that in a remote period of Southwestern prehistory there were only one or two recognized

Kokopelli effigy pitcher (ca. AD 1000-1150)

deities, and that the pantheon increased as the Pueblo culture became more complex. The God of Fire and the Humpbacked Flute Player could very well be the oldest in concept among Southwestern archaelogical supernaturals.

Mural painting within ceremonial kiva chambers appears to date back to A.D. 1000. Considering his appearance in rock and ceramic art, it is not surprising to discover that the omnipresent Flute Player is represented on kiva murals as well. Two such murals in Chaco Canyon portray Kokopelli. An eleventh century kiva shows a flute player within a hunting scene that includes archers and mountain sheep. Another kiva scene, probably from the thirteenth century, features three fluteplayers painted in red on a white background. A phallic humpback associated with a female figure is illustrated on an Awatovi mural, probably a fertility reference. Just these few examples reiterate the theme so characteristic of Kokopelli in other ancient images: he changes shape to suit the need.

CONCLUSION

The popular contemporary image of the Humpbacked Flute Player shares with the Kokopelli of old the unresolved mysteries of his origin, development, role, and ultimately, his meaning. Novelists and poets take delight in such ambiguity, since a character who eludes facts invites the imagination to ponder his, possibilities, thus providing a fitting subject for artistic and creative freedom.

Like the Anasazi and early Pueblo artists or shamans who etched Kokopelli's many shapes on rock walls, and like the ancestors who developed ceremonies and rituals to dramatize his spiritual roles, today's artists and artisans may take advantage of Kokopelli's enigmatic character by giving their imaginations free rein to embody his numerous roles and multifaceted personality. The ceremonial Kokopelli of Robert Montoya, personifying the elemental relationship of humans to their world in the dance of this priestly and sometimes ghostly figure, pay homage to ancient tradition even as they display the colors and forms of a very contemporary imagination.

ROBERT MONTOYA, PUEBLO PAINTER

by James T. Bialac

Robert Montoya was born into a family of artists. His grand-mother, Crucita Trujillo Cruz of San Juan Pueblo, was an award-winning potter who exhibited in the nationwide Pottery Exposition in Syracuse, New York in 1941. Juan A. Montoya of Sandia Pueblo, Bob's father, married her daughter, Geronima Cruz Montoya. Geronima was a student under Dorothy Dunn at the Santa Fe Indian School, where she later became a teacher of painting from 1935 through 1961. She is a wonderful painter in her own right, and her talent has passed on to her children.

Bob's brother Paul, also a painter, is well known for his minia-ture figures in large dance and ceremonial scenes. Paul is presently Chief of Police of Laguna Pueblo, and Bob, like his brother, has a foot in both worlds. He presently employed by the Bureau of Indian Affairs. He began his painting career in 1970, the same year he started his Masters Degree in Regional and City Planning.

Geronima Cruz Montoya can be classified as a traditionalist, but Bob is hard to tie down. His architectural background shows in many of his paintings. Some are done in a traditional mode and some in a contemporary manner, and many combine the two styles. The originality with which he portrays the well known Pueblo art subjects sets him apart from the present Pueblo artists. Unlike Helen Hardin, he did not seek an independent style of painting, but his work is immediately identifiable and highly collectable. His original paintings are in great demand.

Living in a white world as he presently does, it is nonethe-less clear that he had a traditional upbringing which tran-scends into his paintings. He has not concentrated on any particular subject, but has shown his knowledge garnered from his Indian upbringing in his paintings on the emer-gence legends of his people, his Kokopelli series, his hunting scenes, and his knowledge of the Kachinas.

Bob can be seen with his mother and brother any August in Santa Fe at the Indian Market, where he has won many awards for his paintings, which are executed in such a clean, precise and understanding manner. He is noticeably above the pack in setting new trends that show his versatility. His sensitivity and understanding of the subjects on which he draws brings a story to almost every painting he completes, whether it is a single figure or a painting with many varied objects, people and animals. Bob has an outgoing and pleasant manner, charming his listeners as he reveals the stories and concepts behind his paintings.

I have been collecting Indian paintings and kachinas since 1964. For many years, I had stopped by Geronima Cruz

Montoya's booth at Indian Market, and in 1972 Bob was there with a few of his paintings. I was immediately interested because he did such beautiful work, and I was fascinated by the way he brought his training in architecture into the compositions.

I have in my own personal collection nine of Bob Montoya's paintings, dating from 1972 to 1992. The most recent work is a 14" x 20" casein watercolor entitled "Emergence at Blue Lake." This painting, which was awarded a Third Place in the 1992 Indian Market, is one of Bob's series of works focusing on the Pueblo emergence myth. It shows four Kachinas emerging from water in the center of a Kiva, advancing towards a ladder which appears to enter a Sipapu (entrance into the world) which is floating in the night sky. Close by the Kachinas is a bowl filled with prayer feathers.

The spiritual message so typical of his work is revealed in a description written on the back:

> "Through the fog, the water seems to move as the cloud deities emerge in the form of tail feathers of the eagle."

SPIRITUALITY IN THE PAINTING OF ROBERT B. MONTOYA

In the 1990's, with divisiveness based on ethnicity, culture, and religious belief so prevalent worldwide that humanity's very existence is threatened, it is essential to understand spirituality as something other than that which divides us. Indeed, "spirituality" is a far broader term than "righteousness" or "religion." It is inclusive rather than exclusive, denoting a central core of harmony, balance, and wholeness that maintains vitality and inner peace. Within a community or society, a spiritual existence requires cooperation and coordination of the parts to serve the whole. To be universal, harmony would have to extend beyond the self and the community to all creatures, to the world, and beyond.

Although human existence has always included elements of conflict and division, many cultures have viewed spirituality as a quality that humans must strive for. Recent research on the human evolution suggests that the species evolved independently in many locations, utterly wiping out similar species competing for food and territory. Recorded history contains ample illustrations of the same phenomenon with respect to our own species. And the daily news is almost certain to feature variations on the theme of strife and discord. In contrast to contemporary trends and ancient facts, the ceremonies expressing spiritual beliefs of the native peoples of the Rio Grande pueblos stand out as extraordinarily gentle, aesthetic and holistic representations of human resilience and harmonious balance with the environment.

In February, 1994, I visited Albuquerque and Santa Fe to discuss the artwork for **Kokopelli Ceremonies** with Robert Montoya. He invited me and several other friends to a Deer Dance at San Juan Pueblo, where his mother, Geronima Cruz Montoya, makes her home. The Deer Dance is a very popular ceremony common to the Rio Grande Pueblos. It is also one of the Native American dances most familiar to the general public, for it is not secret, mysterious, or esoteric. The celebration of the Deer Dance is communal and social. During and after the dance, guests who have come for the dance are invited to a feast in a Pueblo home. The Montoya feast was indeed wonderful, entertaining perhaps sixty guests in a small space within just a few hours.

More wonderful than the feast was an event such as I had never witnessed in any community where I have lived: the entire male population of San Juan, aged four or five to early twenties, congregated and danced for the entire day. Having spent twenty-five years living with or in some way relating to this age group as godfather, teacher, adviser, coach, and counselor, I was amazed at the energy and communal cohesiveness that kept these boys and young men in the plaza all day, their dancing appreciated and enjoyed by family members and many other well-wishers from outside the Pueblo. It was a lesson in human contact and spirituality: the boys and young men in their ceremonial garb, the witnesses, the blue sky above, the forest beyond—all seemed unified and harmonized by the singer's voice and the rhythm of the drums.

Unlike many of the Indian Nations that were displaced by the white man, the Pueblos of the Rio Grande valley have maintained their ties with the land of their forefathers. For almost three thousand years, the Four Corners region was home to the Anasazi, the "ancient ones," who are believed to have been the ancestors of today's Pueblos. While many Plains tribes and even the geographically close Navajos and Apaches endured forced migrations, the Pueblo Nations maintained their geographic roots in their ancestral homes, assimilating parts of Spanish and Anglo culture while continuing to maintain their ceremonial traditions.

Robert Montoya's art manifests a profound identification with Pueblo culture and a deep veneration of Pueblo ceremonial practices. In his theme and subject matter, he continually explores the relationship of humans to the cosmos, utilizing traditional Pueblo imagery in conjunction with a very contemporary sense of color, design and composition. The Kokopelli series superbly expresses this juxtaposition of ancient and modern by featuring traditional pottery motifs and ceremonial dress, yet emphasizing the geometrical abstraction of Kokopelli's form and often the translucency of his presence in a fashion unattainable in traditional two-dimensional representations.

In many of Montoya's paintings, the technique is primarily two-dimensional, with limited three-dimensional perspective and shading, yet another more ethereal dimension, which might be referred to as "hyperspace," is suggested by the intersection of curved surfaces. Some paintings, such as "Deer Night Sky," combine all three distinctive spaces. The abstract step design is primarily two dimensional, except where a curved surface separates one area into two shades and another curve distorts the linear regularity of the pattern. The deer antlers are shaded three-dimensionally, and a sense of depth is created by their stark contrast to the night sky. The center of the image presents the spiritual hyperspace in which the kachina manifests.

Color and texture as well as spatial illusion are used to convey spiritual presence and the relationship among the three worlds. The two-dimensional plane is rendered in earth colors, while the three-dimensional world is black and white. The sharp contrast of the antlers against the sky is softened by the delicate texture of the feathers.

Brilliant color in the kachina mask draws attention to the translucent dimension from which this figure emanates. At the same time, the mask integrates and harmonizes the earth tones of the lower world with the blacks and whites of the upper world. The overall impression conveyed is a harmonious integration of opposites, for which the viewer needs no special knowledge of Pueblo culture, since the impact of form, color and composition is sufficient to establish this feeling.

Deer Night Sky

The cosmic or spiritual dimension is presented in many of the Kokopelli paintings, usually in terms of swirling bands of color or intersecting curves that may indicate movement, a rainbow-like apparition, the roundness of a kiva, or the roughness of a rock surface. The transparency or translucency of Kokopelli, his feathers, or the pottery, emphasizes the non-materiality of the world from which he proceeds. Even without background about Kokopelli or explanations of Pueblo beliefs and practices, the ethereal quality of this spiritual dimension creates an immediate impact, making it clear that something sacred is happening.

Another spiritual theme that Montoya frequently revisits in his work is the Emergence. In the creation myths of the Rio Grande Pueblos, the story is told of emergence from the underworld, usually from a lake, followed by migration and dispersion. "Emergence from Blue Lake" uses color and form variation to emphasize the introduction of spirituality to earth. As they emerge, the spirit-beings bring brilliant color and sharp, dramatic form into a world which previously consisted only of the soft shapes and earth colors of the kiva and the contrasting black and white of the night sky.

By choosing the moment of emergence, Montoya simultaneously emphasizes a beginning, an ongoing process, and the

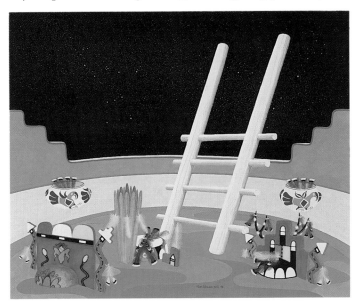

Emergence from Blue Lake

mystery and spirituality of the spirit-beings, who are shown only through their tablitas. They are led by the chieftain-priest, who will ascend the kiva ladder ahead of the spirits of clouds and rain, thunder and lightning, and the deer. The spiritual dimension from which these figures emerge is portrayed by stylized color variation in the lake, in contrast to the normal shading of the ladder, which represents the way into the world. By depicting the Emergence as taking place within a kiva, Montoya implies a correspondence between the original creation story and contemporary Pueblo ceremonial observances, in which the rain gods ascend from within the kiva.

The Gathering of the Rain People

A different moment in time during the Emergence is highlighted in "The Gathering of the Rain People," where the final three Rain People arise from the water as those who have already emerged await their departure to the pueblos. The quality of mystery is emphasized by the shadowy outlines of the Rain People, while the spirituality of the moment is established by subtle variations in hue and lighting rather than dramatic color. The shadows of the Rain People are distinguished by white flecks, their resemblance to the night sky suggesting that they share its cosmic power. Various tablitas appear in outline from the central shadow, conveying an impression of individuality developing out of and deriving its energy from a unified spirit. This vision is consistent with Montoya's focus on the ceremonial forces at the heart of Pueblo life that unite the individual with the community.

Variations on a theme, such as kachinas, Kokopelli, or Emergence, enable Montoya to celebrate the wonderful diversity embodied in the creation and development of spiritual life. The latitude and depth of Montoya's spiritual vision, however, is exemplified by a single major work completed in 1994, titled "We See Yet Do Not Understand." Theme, composition, color, and numerous traditional elements combine to present a world simultaneously reflecting both fragmentation and harmony. In a commentary on the work, Montoya states that the composition of several paintings illustrates that "we often lose focus on reality, and distractions

We See Yet Do Not Understand

in life often lead to our inability to acquire harmony within ourselves."

The central image, a large rainbird pottery bowl depicted three-dimensionally, radiates a series of images painted two dimensionally, as if on a flat storyboard, but seen in perspective nonetheless by virtue of variation in background color. The pottery represents the spirit and soul of both man and woman. The ladder extending to the universe symbolizes humans' quest for harmony. In the words of the artist, "Radiating in four sacred directions are the roads of life, one of which we must select and travel. All are good roads; however, some are longer and more difficult to travel. The serpent guides our journey as it gracefully moves among the rocks and crevices of the road." The road of the serpent Avanyu, painted in the traditional black-on-black of San Ildefonso pottery, represents spiritual or cosmic space.

The four seasons are shown clockwise: starting at the upper right, spring is portrayed by the rain gods awaiting their opportunity to emerge and bring new life and hope, summer by the rainbow and the ceremonial dance figures, fall by the flowers and the ceremonial deer hunt, and winter by the deer dance figures and the kiva. Above the kiva, awaiting their

time of appearance, are the guardians of the Pueblo life ways. Their power and strength is symbolized by the lightning.

While the artist's commentary helps in appreciating the intent and the story behind the painting, it is immediately evident from a study of this work that it represents spiritual forces. The powerful sky, the masks, the ceremonial costumes, the detailed abstractions, and the overlapping spaces all point to a symbolic cycle, which is further reinforced by the circular and curved elements of the design. The color combinations (black and white, muted earth colors, and areas of brilliant color with dramatic contrasts) amplify the spiritual vision of a wholeness that integrates and harmonizes extraordinary diversity. Robert Montoya's spirituality, expressed in these paintings, is one highly creative individual expression of the Pueblo tradition of veneration for life, understood as a privileged struggle of the human spirit for balance and harmony in the universe.

Kokopelli
ceremonies

KOKOPELLI'S SUNRISE SONG

The first rays of dawn bring the beauty, strength and wonderful power of the sun to the world of humans. The rising sun creates vibrant light throughout the universe, illuminating the earth, the sky, the stars, just as a painter illuminates the world by trying colors just to see what happens. The cosmic light show that results is a happy accident, the backdrop for the song and dance that we celebrate as life.

Kokopelli summons and hails the sunrise. The sun's warmth and creative power is the music that announces the day and causes life on earth to develop and increase. The sun brings fruitfulness to the harvest and to all enterprises.

In the morning, the Pueblo people go outside to pray to the rising sun, to seek power and strength to accomplish the goal for the day. They pray for the wellbeing of their family, their pueblo, and humankind, acknowledging that we are not the only ones here on this earth, that we were placed here for some important reason, that we are supposed to be part of something. Just as the sun rises daily, the prayer to the sun for the power and strength to understand and accomplish our purpose occurs daily for our entire life.

The pottery bowl reminds us, that life is really never complete. Life is never perfect until it has closed, symbolized by the gap in the line encircling the bowl at the top. Perfectionism and rigidity are ways to "paint yourself into a corner" and lose the spirit of vitality represented by music and ceremonial dancing. White turkey feathers softened by eagle down portray the breath of life.

Translucent, Kokopelli floats above the earth, allowing the universe to pass through. The stars on his legs represent the morning and evening stars, and the stars on his body are symbols of the warrior who seeks strength from morning and evening stars in order to protect and defend his people. On the earth, the stars represent the two clans of the Tewas, black for summer and white for winter. The entire cosmos reverberates to Kokopelli's sunrise song.

Soe-Khuwa-pin 93.

39

KOKOPELLI'S GIFT TO THE SUN

The Pueblo people pray in the morning, speaking to the sun as a father. Kokopelli's prayer includes both petition and gratitude, acknowledging the power and strength generated by the sun and shared by the people, asking the sun daily, "Grant me the strength that you have, the power that you've generated to this world, that makes things grow and live."

The life force is symbolized by the pottery bowl Kokopelli is carrying. Pottery embodies the four elements—earth and water mixed and fired to a hard finish, filled with the spirit at life, the invisible force that keeps us alive and preserves harmony in the world.

Presenting this pot full of his life, Kokopelli makes an offering: "I grant you my life for the life you have given me." The rainbird is the messenger who, by flying close to the sun, will make sure the sun receives the gift presented through this beautiful pot.

Kokopelli's two humps carry all that is given us to bear, both good and evil. Kokopelli prays, "Grant me the strength to bear all that you have given me, both my happiness and my trials and tribulations. You've granted me the strength that I've asked for many, many times, to get me through a day, help me through a ceremony, carry me through a life, and for all that you've granted me, I present you my life."

The patterns on Kokopelli's humps and kilt are based on Tewa manta designs representing clouds and lightning. These motifs are often found as a wainscot a few feet above the floor of a kiva, or ceremonial chamber. Contained within the decorative manta, the burdens of Kokopelli's life are held within something beautiful that represents the completeness of male and female, lightning and clouds, line and circle, pain and pleasure, movement and stasis.

Though Kokopelli carries no flute, the musical elements of song and dance are suggested by the shells around his waist and the dancing movement of his feet as he presents the pot. The circle is completed as Kokopelli presents the pottery bowl to the rising sun.

Soe-Khuwa-pín 93.

KOKOPELLI BROTHERS

Kokopelli images in pictographs and petroglyphs are remarkably varied: he is sometimes depicted as a single figure, but just as often with others of his own kind or among several other figures that may be human, animal, insect or plant. He varies widely in size, shape, and role. While students of ethnography have been able to trace stylistic and regional similarities, it remains a matter of speculation who or what Kokopelli was.

This image invites the viewer to participate imaginatively in the guessing game about Kokopelli. One Kokopelli could be larger than the other, or perhaps one is in the foreground and one is in the background. One figure may be standing on the ground while the other is in the air, or possibly that illusion is a matter of perspective. By playing with the idea of Kokopelli figures on a rock surface, the painting underscores the ambiguity surrounding the Humpback's significance. The speculative nature of interpretation is further emphasized by the curved instrument each holds—is it a musical instrument, a wand or a staff?

Many of the legends and stories about Kokopelli as well as much of the rock art emphasize that he wasn't alone. He was very likely a member of a society or a clan, and clan members typically recognize one another as being brothers. The sense of brotherhood extended beyond individual pueblos into the major language groups (Tewa, Tiwa, Towa and Keres), so that members of a particular society or clan from different pueblos usually acknowledged a common bond.

Community and spiritual concord, symbolized in most of the other paintings by pottery, is embodied in the corn plant. The life of the pueblo is centered on the sustenance represented by the corn, and much of ceremonial life is made up of rituals that emphasize rain, fertility, and plentiful life. Because survival in the Pueblo lands was dependent primarily on success of crops, the importance of corn to the life of the people could hardly be overemphasized. And yet we can also see by the geometric, stepwise design of the corn plant (imitated from an ancient rock drawing in Galisteo) that corn is also representative of something greater, the spirit of common purpose or brotherhood.

Soe-Khuwa-pin 92.

Kokopelli's Sacred Prayers

For the Pueblo people, prayers are requests not for material things, but for something that is good for everybody, such as health, happiness, harmony, good harvest, more game, increased strength, or good judgment to make a decision. These supplications are symbolized by the turkey feathers, one of the most important feathers for the Tewas.

In a ceremony common to the Pueblos, the feathers are ceremonially smoked with tobacco. Kokopelli, taking on the role of a priest or emissary of the people, is blowing into the pot, smoking the feathers so that they may be purified and cleansed. At the culmination of the ceremony, the pot with all the feathers will be taken out of the pueblo and placed as an offering. Pervaded by the smoke, the feathers now embody all that was said and sung over them, all the requests made by the people. The beauty of the pottery bowl signifies that all the supplications are for something that will enhance the beauty and harmony of life.

That harmony is manifested in the patterns within the painting: the triangle patterns from the pottery are picked up in Kokopelli's kilt and manta; sky colors are reflected in his kilt; and the circularity of the pot is imitated not only by Kokopelli's humped back, but also by the sweep and flow of his body as it moves in dance. Music, dance, and the harmony of the elements are also symbolized by the tassels on the kilt and sash, decorative portrayals of clouds and rain.

This is a ceremony with a stylized sky as a backdrop. The movement in the background indicates the winds, which will carry the ceremonial smoke of the people's petitions to whichever of the directions is most conducive to answering each prayer. Nature herself, assisted by Kokopelli as priest, becomes the messenger for the prayers of the people.

Soe-Khuwa-pín 93.

DANCE OF THE KOKOPELLI

Pueblo ceremonies are typically conducted either in the village plaza or in the ceremonial kiva. There is nothing quiet or static about a kiva ceremony: it's full of excitement, motion, and emotion, as manifested by the dancing Kokopelli. Movement is indicated by the doubled image and even lighter shadow image in the background of each figure. Purpose and meaning within the ceremonial performance are inseparable from its realization in music and dance.

Brownish earth colors in the background are reminiscent of rock surfaces on which the Anasazi, ancestors of the Pueblos, incised and painted numerous and widely diverse images of the Humpback Flute Player. The vitality of the dance and the variation in costume point to the shapeshifting character of Kokopelli, who has been depicted throughout the Four Corners area in a variety of roles, whether musician, priest, fertility god, or warrior. As celebrants in this kiva ritual, they partake in several of these roles simultaneously.

Tewa pueblos are made up of two clans, the Winter people and the Summer people. The father's side determines which clan an individual is born into, and society within each Tewa pueblo has evolved from the two clans. Identification as a clan member is a matter of pride, so that frequently competitions and contests occur between the clans. The white pottery bowl on the left represents the Winter clan, and the black bowl on the right stands for the Summer clan. Just as the Summer and Winter people make up the totality of the pueblo, so the Summer and Winter seasons express the polarities of the yearly life cycle. Dancing together emphasizes the concordance of the opposites.

Symmetry and balance within the image signify the harmonious interweaving of seasons to make a year and the harmonious interrelationship of the people through clan participation. Within a relatively narrow range of earth colors, this image demonstrates the arts of pottery, costume, song and dance in their limitless variability of style, form and design. Art holds a mirror to life as the subtle variations within the image imitate the infinite variability among humans that allows for diversity within the unified fabric of our lives.

Soe-Khuwa-piñ 92.

ARROW PRIEST

Arrows for the Pueblo people signify strength, power and resistance to evil. Certain Pueblo societies demonstrate their curing abilities and eliminate any disbelief in these abilities by swallowing arrows. Curing or medicine is both physical and psychological, and good health is consistent with being in balance within oneself, with the community, and with the universe.

Ceremonies held at night are remarkable for their intensity, for the night sky highlights the mystery and ceremonialism of the performance while the stars are powerful and silent witnesses to the human demonstration of prowess. Thus harmony with the universe rather than power over nature is emphasized.

Another reason for ceremonies being held at night is that during the Spanish occupation, many of the Pueblo spiritual observances were not allowed to be held in public, and thus rituals were performed in secret, often at night. Because of the legacy of interference with their religious expressions, certain observances, particularly those most associated with power and curing, have gone underground and cannot be witnessed by non-Pueblos. Other ceremonies continue to be open to the public but are traditionally performed at night.

One of the best vantage points for viewing a ceremony is to be perched on top of one of the Pueblo buildings or atop the kiva. One is surrounded by darkness while experiencing the feeling of observing from a height, from a special place within the Pueblo. The backdrop could also be a circular wall within the kiva, with the Pueblo represented by painting on the wall and the night sky above. The reddish circle on which Kokopelli dances is the terracotta clay typical of the Southwest and commonly found in the Pueblos.

The clay color radiates through Kokopelli's body painting and ceremonial dress, and flows into the rainbird on the ceremonial pot. An intense square in the middle of Kokopelli's body signifies the heartline or lifeline, indicating that he is of the earth. Earth, air, water and fire intermingle harmoniously, from the ground of clay, through the breath of feathers and the rainbird messenger to the clouds, to the fire of lightnings in Kokopelli's kilt and the arrows swallowed by the Arrow Priest.

Soe-Khuwa-pin 94.

RAINBIRD PRIEST

Rain is essential to the life of the people. It supports the life of crops, animals, and humans, and therefore is a dominant influence in song and dance, costume and design. Many Pueblo stories and legends speak of the clouds themselves as the gods because they bring the moisture that generates plant and animal life.

Kokopelli as Rainbird Priest represents a high-ranking individual in a pueblo performing a specific ceremony to summon rain. Kokopelli is playing music into the bowl, which features the traditional Zia representation of the rainbird, messenger to the clouds. The bowl itself represents the pueblo, and by extension, the world. The Rainbird Priest's music and dance inspires the rainbird to summon rain from the clouds, so that the pot may be filled.

The warm golds and tans of the background are the hues of an indoor ceremonial chamber, indicating that the ceremony is being performed indoors. The circular pattern suggests that the ritual is being celebrated with great vigor. At the same time the roundness expresses the wholeness of the moment, the cycle wherein human breath, fired earth, and rain combined generate the totality of life.

Ceremonial costume evokes the harmony between nature and the people, for whom the priest is the mediator. Kokopelli is painted in traditional warrior colors and star symbols, wearing a kilt, sash and blanket. The white lines on the face and the white crosses are symbols of the warrior, whose strength is vital for the survival of the people. The turkey feathers adorning the kilt and blanket represent his prayers of supplication.

Even though the figure is contemporary, the integration of form and function and the harmonious blending of shape, color and symbolism is typical of the spiritual nature of traditional Pueblo art. Even the presentation of Kokopelli's face, where the hairline meets the face in a step effect, carries the symbolism of rain, wherein the red of the clouds meets the black of the night sky. The curves of Kokopelli's body blend harmoniously with the spherical background and ceremonial pottery.

Soe-Khuwa-pīn 92.

KIVA RAIN PRIEST

Brown and reddish adobe earth tones illustrate the floor of the kiva, the chamber in which certain religious ceremonies are performed and others are prepared for. Intersecting arcs of blue and yellow indicate the circularity of the chamber. These earth and sky colors are also reflected in Kokopelli's face, where red, yellow, brown and blue represent the four directions, north, south, east and west.

Geometric figures dominate this image, with lines, bands, squares, crosses, diamonds, and terraced patterns adorning Kokopelli's body, while his arched posture imitates the roundness of the earth and the kiva chamber. An illusion of movement, created by the sweep of the intersecting arcs near the center of the painting, particularly the headdress, underscores the energetic dynamism of the celebrant.

The reddish square framed with white represents Kokopelli's spirit or life, which is of the earth. It is equivalent to the heartline sometimes depicted in deer or antelope in ceremonial hunting scenes. Above it, the terraced pattern imitates the pattern of steps typically found ascending and descending into the kiva. The steps of the kiva represent the transition to spirituality, to identification with the vitality that holds humans and nature in balance.

Spirituality is mysterious, just barely evading human understanding, like Kokopelli, who cannot be pinned down to a single identity. Thus the Humpback Flute Player is portrayed as a priest, an embodiment of the contact point between the spiritual and material worlds. In this image, the boundary between the Rain Priest's body and the interplay of light and shadow is deliberately left ambiguous, just as the translucency of the pottery bowls implies the interpenetration of the two worlds.

The rainbird, depicted in two different forms on the bowls, is a messenger to the clouds, and like the Rain Priest, represents communication between the material and spiritual worlds. In the Southwest home of the Pueblos, arid much of the year, rain is essential to a life which has traditionally been based on successful agriculture. The Rain Priest, by this kiva ceremony, prays for the nourishment and sustenance of plant, animal and human life.

Soe-khuwa-piñ 93.

SNAKE PRIESTS

Avanyu, the sacred serpent of the Pueblos, is a very powerful symbol of the four basic elements, earth, water, air and fire. In some legends, the serpent is seen as the main body of the earth. Thus, when an earthquake occurs, Pueblo religious leaders may comment that "the serpent has turned over." Other legends present Avanyu as the sacred water serpent who provides power and life to Mother Earth.

The arrow at the end of the tongue is a symbol of lightning power, as seen in the lightning of summer storms, flashing fire through the air as a harbinger of the much-needed rain that supports fertility of plant and animal life, and thus supports human life.

The four elements are also embodied in the pottery bowl, made of earth mixed with water, fired to hardness, and encircling air. The translucency of the bowl creates a three-dimensional effect that suggests floating, indicating an ethereal or spiritual presence.

The Snake Priests, representing the Summer (black) and Winter (white) clans of the Tewas, also appear to be floating above the earth. They embody an awareness of spirituality, the existence of a totality that transcends and permeates the material world, a oneness that is difficult to understand, to bear with, and to live.

That wholeness is represented at the center by the diamond where the Kokopelli's hair intersects, by the pottery bowl, and by the convergence of intersecting arcs, bringing together day and night, earth and sky, the Summer People and the Winter People. Graphically, the painting presents this unity and harmony through color gradations from terracotta through white, indicating a blending of the polar opposites, a spiritual attunement.

Music and dance are evoked by the flute-playing and dancing posture of the Kokopellis, supplying a dimension of movement to enhance the three-dimensional form. Yet even while geometric symmetry and color harmony dominate, the imperfection of material life is represented by the slight asymmetry of day and night, the gap in the uppermost line of the pottery bowl, and the incompleteness of Avanyu, who is nearly, but not quite, joined from head to tail.

Soe-Khawa-pin 94.

RAIN BEARERS

We often see the rainbow and its colors after rainstorms that pass through the pueblos. It is sometimes said that the rainbow, appearing after the nurturing rain has brought life to earth, is a demonstration that the prayers of the people have been received and answered. The rainbow has always symbolized harmony, for its colors are the natural colors of the spectrum.

The Kokopelli represent the sacred Cloud People, the bearers of rain, messengers from the Great Spirit to whom the people are praying, asking for rain to nourish their life. Their translucency is an indication that they are spiritual and very special. The most tangible element of their dress is feathers, which represent the prayers of the Pueblo people for rain.

The Kokopelli are dancing and bearing the sacred water in pottery bowls, which represent clouds. Among the Pueblos, pots are the means by which sacred water is dispensed in ceremonials, and here each bowl carries a symbolic meaning in its design. The feather design stands for the prayers of the people, for feathered creatures rise from the earth to the clouds, and thus are suitable messengers for supplications.

The middle pot depicts Avanyu, the sacred water serpent, whose tongue represents the power of lightning. The bowl on the right features a simple lightning design, for lightning is the harbinger of summer rainstorms in the Pueblo area.

The top background suggests the rays of the sun through the sky and through the clouds. The arc below the rainbow represents the earth. The dance of the Kokopelli or Cloud People signifies the gentle touching of the earth by the first drops of rain, just as the subtle movements of Pueblo dancers imitate the natural events they are intended to call forth.

The realization of the people's prayers in the appearance of the Cloud People conveys the message that they are living in harmony with the earth and therefore deserve the nurturing rain. While rain is emphasized, it is clear that the harmony of all four elements is essential to spiritual wholeness. Within the ethereal presentation of the Kokopelli, pottery and the dancing ground embody earth, airy feathers carry the people's requests, water is borne in response to prayers, and fire is evident in the sun's rays and lightning symbols.

Soe-Khuwa-pin '94.

SUN FATHER

In some historical depictions of Kokopelli, he is shown with a staff rather than a flute. As Sun Father, he carries a staff representing his authority, just as the cane given by the state or federal government embodies the authority of Pueblo Governors.

As is typical of the nonviolent attitude of the Pueblos towards power, Kokopelli uses his authority in a subtle way that accentuates the harmonious rhythms of nature. He is stepping slowly and softly from day to night, gently walking into the evening without disturbing the moon's sleep.

Thus his authority is the serene power of nature, wherein the dominion of the sun is replaced by that of the moon, inevitably and without question, as the sun goes to its normal rest. In a larger sense, this movement may be seen as representative of the life cycle.

The ceremonial pots represent sun and moon. The lightning design of the pot on the left emphasizes the sun's fiery power, while the shading of the pot on the right resembles the actual shading we observe on the moon, which does not provide its own source of light, but simply reflects the light of the sun.

The progress of the Sun Father may be interpreted in terms of the daily cycle of day and night. It may also be regarded as emblematic of the resting of Father Sun during the winter solstice. The importance of this time of year is commemorated by all the Pueblos to acknowledge and offer respect to the sun, who rests after giving us his life and energy throughout the year.

For most Pueblos during this time no meetings are held, no dancing takes place, and everybody is asked not to clean house or make noise outside the house in deference to the sun, who is asleep and deserves respect and consideration. Thus the wholeness and natural cycling of life are emphasized by giving restfulness the same importance, power and authority as the vigorous activity we usually associate with the Sun.

Soe-Khuwa-pin '94.

UNIVERSAL HARMONY

Harmony is a result of continual balanced living among all things on earth and between earth itself and the elements. The Pueblos interpret abundance of crops and animal life as an indication that they are living in harmony with universal laws, for the balanced coexistence of humans, new plants and animals insures survival and quality of life.

The colors surrounding Kokopelli's ceremonial dance are traditionally associated with the four directions: black represents north; red, east; turquoise, south; and yellow, west. The central white traditionally represents the zenith and also is typically identified with moisture. Thus Kokopelli is shown dancing at the center of the universe, maintaining concord through his music and dancing even as he warns of discord.

The symbol of warning issued by Kokopelli is a way to draw attention to the need for humans to recognize that they are only a part of the ecosystem. Humans should realize that the harmony granted to them is governed by their beliefs and values, the capacity to seek peace within oneself and to coexist side by side with one another, with animal and plant life, and with the universe and its elements. The handprint is a warning that these harmonious interrelationships are disappearing, and that as a result, not only the quality of life but survival itself is being threatened.

Humans have always struggled to live harmoniously with one another, with differences in race and religious background, but we see more often today that peaceful coexistence is not succeeding because we have not made a conscientious effort to sacrifice nor been willing to live peaceably with one another.

The feathers on Kokopelli's head and at the end of the flute are turkey feathers, which are used in ceremonies to represent the petitions of the people, messages delivered to the Great Spirit requesting the elemental necessities of life—heat and moisture, abundance of food, ability to lead a life in balance with the elements.

Kokopelli's translucency illustrates the mysteriousness and spirituality of what he is, was, or may have been. Here is something we see through but cannot see, something we want to touch but cannot. We are unable to comprehend or fully realize what Kokopelli's meaning is, other than to appreciate that he offers something intangible and elemental, essential and integral, emanating from the core of existence, the "still point of the turning world."

Soe-Khuwa-Pin '94.

A KOKOPELLI BIBLIOGRAPHY

Albert, Joyce M., "A New Look at the Humpback Flute Player in Anasazi Rock Art," **American Indian Art,** 17, 1: 49-57 (Winter, 1991).

Fewkes, J.W., "Hopi Katcinas," **Twenty-First Annual Report,** Bureau of American Ethnology, Washington, 1903, 13-126.

Field, Clark, **Indian Pottery of the Southwest, Post-Spanish Period,** Philbrook, unpaged.

Gill, Sam D. and Sullivan, Irene F., **Dictionary of Native American Mythology,** Santa Barbara, 1992.

Hawley, Florence M., "Kokopelli of the Prehistoric Southwest Pueblo Pantheon," **American Anthropologist,** 39,4 (Part I): 644-6 (October-December, 1937).

Kidder, A.V. and Guernsey, S.J., "Archaeological Exploration in Northwestern Arizona," *Bulletin 65, Bureau of American Ethnology,* Washington, 1919.

Lambert, Marjorie F., "A Kokopelli Effigy Pitcher from Northwestern New Mexico," **American Antiquity,** 32, 3: 398-401 (July, 1967).

Lambert, Marjorie F., "A Rare Stone Humpbacked Figurine from Pecos Pueblo, New Mexico," **El Palacio,** 64, 3-4; 93-108 (1957).

Matthews, Washington, **Navajo Legends,** Boston, Houghton Mifflin, 1897.

Parsons, Elsie Clews (ed.), **Hopi Journal of Alexander M. Stephen,** Columbia University Contributions to Anthropology, Vol. 23, 1936.

Parsons, Elsie Clews, "The Humpbacked Flute Player of the Southwest," **American Anthropologist,** 40, 2: 337-8 (April-June, 1938).

Payne, Richard W., **The Hopi Flute Ceremony,** Oklahoma City, Toubat Trails, 1993.

Renaud, Etienne B., "Kokopelli, A Study in Pueblo Mythology," **Southwest Lore,** 14, 2: 25-40 (September, 1948).

Ricks, J. Brent and Anthony, Alexander E., **Kachinas: Spirit Beings of the Hopi.** Avanyu, 1993.

Roberts, Frank H.H., Jr., Bulletin 111, *Bureau of American Ethnology,* Smithsonian, Washington (1932).

Salter, John K., "A Comparison of Two Fertility Figures," **Monument**, 1: 16-24 (Winter, 1960).

Sando, Joe S., **Pueblo Nations: Eight Centuries of Pueblo Indian History**. Santa Fe, NM, Clear Light, 1992.

Schaafsma, Polly, **Indian Rock Art of the Southwest**, School of American Research, Southwest Indian Arts Series, Santa Fe, 1980.

Slifer, Dennis and Duffield, James, **Kokopelli: Flute Player Images in Rock Art**. Santa Fe, NM, Ancient City Press, 1994.

Titiev, Mischa, "Story of Kokopelli," **American Anthropologist**, 41: 91-98, 1939.

Voth, H.R., **The Traditions of the Hopi**, Publication, Field Columbian Museum, Anthropological Series, 6, 8: 220, 1905.

Weaver, Jr., Donald E. "Images on Stone: The Prehistoric Rock Art of the Colorado Plateau," **Plateau**, 55, 2 (1984).

Wellman, Klaus F., "Kokopelli of Indian Paleology," **Journal of the American Medical Association**, 212, 10: 1678-82 (June 8, 1970).

Wellman, Klaus F., "Die Metamorphosen des Kokopelli," **Deutsche**, 95, 10: 532-9 (March 6, 1970).

Wright, Barton, **Hopi Kachinas**. Flagstaff, AZ, Northland, 1977.

Wright, Barton, "The Search for Kokopelli," **Arizona Highways**, 69,7: 14-17 (July, 1993).

Young, John V., **Kokopelli, Casanova of the Cliff Dwellers**. Palmer Lake, CO, Filter Press, 1990.

Young, John V., "Peregrinations of Kokopelli," **Westways** 57,9: 39-41 (September, 1965).

ABOUT THE AUTHOR

Stephen W. Hill is a clinical psychologist in Diamond Bar, California. A graduate of Harvard, he obtained his Ph.D. at the University of Southern California. Prior to his career as a psychologist, he taught English literature and writing for seventeen years in high school and college. Since 1986, he and his family have travelled extensively in New Mexico and Arizona, pursuing their interest in Indian art and culture. Dr. Hill is an avid collector of Native American paintings and a supporter of Native museums, including the National Museum of the American Indian, the Institute of American Indian Arts, the Heard and the Wheelwright. He has published articles on Joe H. Herrera and Ha-So-De.

ABOUT THE ILLUSTRATOR

Robert B. Montoya spent his first thirteen years on the campus of the Santa Fe Indian School, where his parents were employed. After graduating from St. Michael's High School in Santa Fe, he attended the University of New Mexico. In 1970, he was awarded a Ford Foundation Fellowship to attend the University of Oklahoma, where he received his Masters Degree in Regional and City Planning. Since 1970, when he began painting professionally, he has won numerous awards for his paintings, which draw on a wealth of sources for their inspiration—his creative imagination, ancient Pueblo art styles, Pueblo life and religious symbolism and ceremonialism. His artwork is signed with his Tewa name, "Soe-khuwa-pin," which translates as "Fog Mountain."